And All These Roads Be Luminous

And All These Roads Be Luminous

Poems Selected and New

Fountaindale Public Library
Bolingbrook, IL
(630) 759-2102

TRIQUARTERLY BOOKS
NORTHWESTERN UNIVERSITY PRESS

Evanston, Illinois

TriQuarterly Books
Northwestern University Press
Evanston, Illinois 60208–4210

Copyright © 1998 by Angela Jackson. Published 1998 by TriQuarterly
Books/Northwestern University Press. All rights reserved.

Printed in the United States of America

ISBN 0–8101–5076-X (cloth)
ISBN 0–8101–5077–8 (paper)

Library of Congress Cataloging-in-Publication Data

Jackson, Angela, 1951–
    And all these roads be luminous : poems selected and new / Angela
Jackson.
        p.   cm.
    ISBN 0-8101-5076-X (cloth : alk. paper). — ISBN 0-8101-5077-8
(paper : alk. paper).
    I. Title.
PS3560.A179A82   1997
811'.54—dc21   97-41969
                                                                                    CIP

The paper used in this publication meets the minimum requirements of the
American National Standard for Information Sciences—Permanence of Paper
for Printed Library Materials, ANSI Z39.48–1984.

For Angeline Robinson Jackson (Mama)
For George Jackson, Sr. (Madaddy), 1921–1993

For my brothers and sisters
   George, Jr., Delores, Rosemary, Prentiss, Sharon, Betty Jean,
   Debra, and Margaret
   and all of theirs

For my mentor under whose eyes I walked out strong into Calamity and Grace
Hoyt Williams Fuller, 1923–1981

Contents

And All These Roads Be Luminous

Dr. Watts Meets the Man with the White Liver

Dark Legs and Silk Kisses

The Midnight Market of Memory and Dream

The God of Fire

Solo in the Boxcar Third Floor E

A House of Extended Families

Poems from FESTAC '77

Acknowledgments

Many of these poems appeared previously in *Black World, The Black Collegian, First World, NOMMO, Obsidian, Hoodoo 7, Callaloo, Mississippi Valley Review, The Chicago Reader, South and West, The Spoon River Quarterly, Okike, The Black Scholar, Essence, Chicago Literary Review, Cumbaya, 15 Chicago Poets, Focus on Writing, Open Places, Harbor Review, Yellow Silk, 13th Moon, River Styx, Black American Literature Forum, The Pushcart Prize: Best of the Small Presses, In Search of Color Everywhere, Mississippi Writers: Reflections of Childhood and Youth, Eyeball, Emergence,* and *TriQuarterly.* My thanks to the editors of these publications, and to their readers so attentive to recall this voice. A special gratitude to the editorial staff of TriQuarterly Books and Northwestern University Press, especially Reginald Gibbons, editor and friend.

In making the selection of poems for this book, I have chosen only a few from *Dark Legs and Silk Kisses* (TriQuarterly Books/Northwestern University Press, 1993), which is in effect a book-length poem sequence, which I hope the reader will consider in full.

VooDoo/Love Magic

I'm gon put a hex on you
work some voo-doo magic
        on
        yo mind.

I'mma mess wid you.

I'm gon set a love tune
        in yo heart
have you singing Me
from morning till noon to
mid/
night. You cain't help
        yoself.
Baby
I'm gon own yo Soul.

Gonna do to you
what you done to me/
        and mo/
. . . wake you up at fo
just to
call my name
    make you see my face/
in yo mirror
    have you hearing my voice/
in the wind
you/
better/
Watch/out

Cuz
     I'm getting
     into yo head—

Ready to do a love thang
to yo in/
     sides
Workin voo-doo on u/Doin Black/
        Woman/Love
        Magic
        to
        U.

(I'm gon put a hex on you

And All These Roads Be Luminous

Strolling

Some places you could die in,

if you could just go on
living there.

The boy, his legs bare and small,
swinging in the stroller, sockless, suede-shoed feet touching
the runner. He can walk, but the woman
keeps him from running
into the street. He won't obey
but listens to everything we say. Head tilted, face changing
with the conversation. Green leaves leap through fences.
Cars wait while we cross. And each bird the boy greets
with its name, "Bird," flies away. The sky holds everything.

The women pushes her son's son along. Her arms strong enough
to hold
nine strong horses prancing.
She's given her money away
because someone had to bury
a child. That is the worst thing.
A mother burying her child.

I would never do that to her, even though it means
what it means.
A thousand years from now
when I am only a dream
I will dream this dream
of strolling.
Perhaps I am doing so now.

Fish Fry: On the Cleaning and Eating of Secrets

for Jacqui

I
At last you pull the fish from the dark lake.
And it is bigger than any lie
we've told.
So big it swallowed you once
and you lived in its belly
for twenty odd years.
I don't believe this.
But it's true.

We've been sitting on this bank
for almost that long,
telling our fish stories
and waiting.
Sun darkening our arms and faces.
All that while
you waited in the lake
like a dream
like a stone.

II
At any time women bring me fish.
Some pulled out of the shallows,
so small I laugh at them and would not
give them my skill, I throw them back
into the lake, deep into its center.

Others I keep,
they wiggle and twist,
want water and gulp air through frightened gills.
Brought to light to die.

III
I am the fishwife
shouting in the marketplace.
The smell of life on my hands
muted by lemon
sliced down the center
and washed over my palms,
between fingers, over wrists, on the backsides.

IV
I clean fish for a living.
It is nasty, smelly work, but vigorous
to slit the devilish things
and pull out the shivering insides,
snap the life strings,
bathing my hands in blood.
I cut off the heads
and trim the sharp fins.
I scrape the scales to skin.

Harsh work if you can do it.

I am alive in the middle of it,
to the wrists.

V
My cousin, eyes cloudy with Canadian Mist,
kept a giant fish in her bathtub.
Like one of the family.
She was in trouble.
And could not kill it.

It worried me.
Unnatural in the house.
And so big.
The bathroom shrank.
It swam,
brushing the curves of the porcelain pool.
Like a shadow come alive.
She had to kill it
or live unclean, hungry.
Servant to a pair of fins.

VI
If need be, catch fish with your bare hands.

VII
Give me your monster from the deep.
I will cut off his head.
I will make him delicious, twelve different ways.
Nothing slips away from women quick as sunlight.
Up to our thighs in the center of things.
Shouting across the water
like well-fed fishwives.

We must have a party, a real fish fry.
Where the meal is delicious and multiplies.
And we search for meat with delicious fingers,
like musicians inside the just-right skin.
We grind the tiny bones between strong teeth.
Not one of us can die, except from laughing.
And there are baskets left over.

VIII

Yet

your monster tests my skill.
I look him in the mouth off and on,
taking him in and out of the icebox.
But he is fresh for days, and his eyes turn to opals.

So courage makes my wrists strict, and love my fingers deft.
I split your demon, gullet to tail
like red ridinghood's woodsman slit the wolf,
and there you toss amid thick blood and reeds like a girl
in a dream
waking to laugh you and
I who am now fishwife
and midwife as well.

IX

But you are hero now. I am witness to the tale.
I have fish of my own to fry.
With your fingernails
you scrape through guts, skin, and scales
or like a prisoner file through bars of flesh and fin.
I believe you.
What you leave will greet surfaces,
skim dark water
like a lily,
like a bubble of air,
like the outfit of the lost child
last seen crying across the lake,
like the shirt of the woman
who sweats naked from the waist
in her kitchen
in full view of fishermen and

women listening to the danger of heat,
the welcome of oils, watching
fish writhe, be gutted clean, then dressed
under the swift sway of sun-darkened breasts,
watching
fish fry.

The Love of Travelers

Doris, Sandra, and Sheryl

At the rest stop on the way to Mississippi
we found the butterfly mired in the oil slick;
its wings thick
and blunted. One of us, tender in the fingertips,
smoothed with a tissue the oil
that came off only a little;
the oil-smeared wings like lips colored with lipstick
blotted before a kiss.
So delicate the cleansing of the wings. I thought the color soft as
    watercolors
would wash off under the method of her mercy for something so slight
and graceful, injured, beyond the love of travelers.

It was torn then, even after her kindest work,
the almost-moth, exquisite charity could not mend
what weighted the wing, melded with it,
then ruptured it in release.
The body of the thing lifted out of its place
between the washed wings.
Imagine the agony of a self separated by gentlest repair.
"Should we kill it?" one of us said. And I said yes.
But none of us had the nerve.
We walked away, the last of the oil welding the butterfly
to the wood of the picnic table.
The wings stuck out and quivered when wind went by.
Whoever found it must have marveled at this.
And loved it for what it was and

had been.
I think, meticulous mercy is the work of travelers,
and leaving things as they are
punishment or reward.

I have died for the smallest things.
Nothing washes off.

Blue Milk

Then we went to Bunny's house behind the church.
And played the Miracles Jesus never did,
over and over, memorizing the whorls of the songs
for the times when we'd know what they meant.
Our fingerprints all over the records, the records all in our prints.
We poured that foreshadowed pain
into our hearts like blue milk
into curved blue bottles with deep stoppers.
Set them in our windows to wait for men who brought love
or not, but thirsty would
lean their fuzzy heads way back
exposing dark, strong necks and,
unstopping stoppers with sweat-staining fingers,
swallow all our blue smokey-miracle milk
till we could count our heart-
beats and breaks
in the deep sinkings and returns
of their adam's apples.

Moment

Each moment is infinite and complete.

After you get up to go and I can think of no more reasons
for you to stay that I can say without making it all too plain,
more plain than what is safe later to look at after we have both
had our way with each other and we don't know yet where to go
with each other or even if we want to, we stand out in front
of the house like proper would-be lovers courting
in an earlier century.
I start staring up at the stars because I want to see a falling star,
and you follow because you have far more experience at stargazing
than I. You are quick and see two, but I see none,
only the after-effect of stars in the vicinity of the falling who talk
in coded light after the one goes down, "Yonder he goes; yonder she
    runs."
This is what I know they say, but you say this is not so
I only think it is
and I say it is so and how do you know
and you say maybe so.
Then you tell me about light, how old it is and how new, how you first
saw time while you sat close by a river that bent; it was then and
it was now is now and it was easier for you to live after that
or was it before
you know it now.
I do too. You have always been standing under this sky with me.
I have always been here somewhere near you.
When you bend down and I arch up, my breasts ending
like starpoints pushing against you,

we make a bow for a moment. You turn your mouth to my cheek and
   say,
"You are beautiful." Then you kiss me.
I look over my shoulder at all those stars and see you.
"You're beautiful."
Now I say that stars that fall are falling in love.
And what do you say then?

My Dream Bo

I am a real character laughing in a cartoon.
In no room for nightmare, tortuous and grim.
My heart pumps up with the dream of him.
I am crazy, sanely crazy as a loon.

Now sorcerous scenarios, quickening winding roads
for magic,
comic,
sexually explicit.

This limber peace eases by lame logic.
It passes all understanding:

O! Now this man's body is a wishbone
in blue overalls.
His long, long legs a long blue bow.
Anatomically a wonder.
O!
I wonder how I'll love him
when light is light or dim.
But I do.
When new air and sky rush through
him. I can see blue bent tender around blue.
O!
The thing that connects him to me must come
out of his throat like a song.

Like
a song.

July 1986
Woodside, California

Joyce Says

Joyce says the man just ain't right.
He got some kinda problem hid outta sight.
And it's making itself known in his peculiar behavior.
O, he present hisself real good first like a saint or savior.
But then the seams start showin
And you be knowin
He tryin to cover up what keep kickin the covers off.

Maybe it stem from a deprived childhood.
Maybe he'd be better if itta would.
Maybe he were ugly and his mama dress him funny.
Maybe everything psychological grow from lack of money.
Joyce says the man just ain't right.
Anyway a wishbone probably got a bonehead jaws tight.
Probably like to ride cows/made up gapped like that.
Probably got ashy legs crusty feet and go to sleep in he hat.
Joyce says you sure you wanna be involved with a individual
who still got the traveling residual
in he physique?

Choosing the Blues

S. Brandi Barnes

When Willie Mae went down to the barber shop
to visit her boyfriend who cut hair there
I went with her. Walking beside her on the street
the men said hey and stopped to watch her just walk.
Boyfriend Barber cut hair and cut his glance at her.
O, he could see the tree for the forest; he pressed
down the wild crest on a man's head and shaved it off
just so he could watch her standing there by the juke
box choosing the blues she would wear for the afternoon.
Right there Little Milton would shoot through the store-
front with the peppermint-stick sentry twirling outside—
"If I didn't love you, baby, grits ain't grocery, eggs
ain't poultry, and Mona Lisa was a man."
And every razor and mouth would stop its dissembling
business. And Time sit down in the barber's chair
and tell Memory poised with its scissors in hand
not to cut it too short, just take a little off the ends.

Chain Gang

The garbage man picks up the shiny black
bags along the curb.
I've seen his powerful arcs, gestures
inside Sam Cooke's voice
the spine itself a "Chain Gang"
a labor fluid
a burdensome grace eased as regular work and pay for it
the heart provoked to love
even the lift
of garbage.

Beauty

How we gathered together to marvel
when the peacocks first came.
We swore we'd love their feathers forever.
Their proud walk we followed with our eyes.
Exclaiming joyfully when they found their way
onto the roof.
Delighted when they took up residence on the deck
and ate the cats' food.
Then the signs descended upon us like creditors:
first the cats ran away
then the blue jays stayed
in the trees
then feathers flew into our faces
and peacock boots marched across the roof
and a peacock general blew us into morning with the
ghastly trumpet in his throat
and a peacock foot soldier left huge drops of stink
where we could sink our footsteps or our eyesight.
Then we began to grumble and call them peahens
after all. Their feathers were not so beautiful.
How had they come to us? We wondered, then knew:
someone like us in love at first sight had dumped
them on our gatestep sometime during the night.
One by one we turned on the cursed birds,
going after them with waterhoses, brooms, bad
words, and evil looks.
Then we looked for bristly sacks and heavy stones and
a way to the ocean.

We began to discuss Sunday dinner, stuffings and fruit,
but this was only psychological warfare,
a coping style under the tyranny of the fowl
who sit on the deck fence
like buzzards, content, and no longer beautiful.

Woodside, California, 1986

Bread

Woke up this morning with The Blues
all around my bed / Tried to eat
my breakfast / Blues all in my bread.
—*Traditional Blues line*

This is the moment between night train whistles.
Bitter the end at the stair of notes.
The blue spaces in the spider's Reconstruction
dream.
That's how you live between paycheck and payment due.

    Your mouth is a flat blue coin purse.
Breath-
less.
Lips spent kisses,
and tongue bankrupt
of bliss.
What air robbed you?

Every bone begs advocate.
Each rib needs a union.
At least conspiracy. Yet
for every sole
and palm—
a callus.

Last night trains whistled and pulled your last reserves
all aboard.

Your hair went on strike.
Nothing's been right, but
your right palm itching.
Then your
left.

You doing these luckless chores
and their children and children's children.
Your hands roughened
by disappointment.
Trace the meaning of that word
in your palm if you will.
You asked for bread.
You could break your teeth on the song of what you got.

The Fitting Room

for Jack LaZebnik and "The Ghost of Senior Hall"

A person has to try on many lives
before she finds one that fits.
    You know what I mean?
People will tell her anything.
How the hat sits too big, and the slip
clings.
She has to be a child again
and see herself in the mirror
in her training bra, in order to dream
                of breasts.
Or like when you shop for shoes
you should do it in the evening
after your feet have swollen
from all your little steps.
The pair you choose then,
sensible and pleasing to foot and eye,
is the pair you will wear
until they wear
out.
I don't know what to make of this.
I don't know what this means,
even though I'm telling it to you.
Like love.
You can choose a man, then choose another,
and all he did was change pants.

But he's the same man in the same life
that didn't fit you, but you tried to squeeze in it
anyway and it was two sizes too small.

People look at you sometimes
and try to have you thinking you'll never find
anything with your measurements.
And you can change those if you want to wear
something bad enough.
Or somebody can cut you down to size.
And you can let them outdo you. Or
leave you in hot water until you draw up.
Then they'll call you country   talk about your trouble
shake their heads and admire how awful you look.
They'll say you a nice person but you got no style.
How does that suit you? Fine. Just fine.
Or

you have to keep taking off garments
and putting other ones on
until you see your self in the seeing glass
as this one has all the glamour and sense you mean
to say what is on your mind.
It looks like it was made with you in mind.
Tell me. You who've lived so long and so little,
        so many lives.
Do you
Do you like this one?

Why I Must Make Language

for Eleanor Hamilton

For
a Voice
like a star.
Shining.
With points to pierce
space,
and be
simple, superb
clarity.
Incandescent.
Some thing
a child might carry
down the black hall,
to make peace with Mystery.
Or woman
into a wooded place
where she may see
the shapes and
names of trees.
Anonymous awe be called
Glory.
Or man
might seek
in the cave
of a woman
and see the writing

on the wall,
and find some
luminosity.
Ancestors may descend
on streams of light.
Or
all look up
and listen
deep
into the night.
The wild
and civilized
Sky.

Ifa as Eve

It was you who released the black bees
of language
from dark red lips 200 thousand years ago.

Who did you talk to, You?
Your husband,
                    good-hearted provider,
could not understand
what was not sigh or yawn or plaintive cry.
Were you lonely inside language?
Odd woman outside the rich abyss of animal pleasure
and discomfit. The tongue finding other bliss—
meaning to educate into a kiss so much later?
You didn't settle for the usual duties,
did you?
Crouching near a tree was not enough. Gathering
the free juice of plums not replete.
Mooning and feeding babies,
washing and breaking wood,
reading stars insufficient.
Oh, they saved it for you, the mute gossip of your tribe
that was not yet tribe till your language bound them
free to seek each other as sisters and brothers. They
peeled the mute memory and used your talk to talk
about you. (Caledonia, Monkeywoman, Mouth.)
Dark woman whose tongue got her in trouble.
Acting unusual and talking back to the dumb.
Whatever you said was poetry.
Everything burst to life from your lips.

Your husband deserted you, didn't he? Too much
terror to take. Unpredictable speech when he wanted
a ride. (Cut the commentary.) You wanted to see stars
and say them. And him you gave a name, and waited
to hear him answer.
When you said Love, he didn't know.
And could not give a vow.
He didn't know how.

Who did you confide in, You?
Your loneliness ice on the red leaf.
You kept quiet after this.
And waited for a kiss.
Someone alone like you.
Talk a wounding wonder sudden.
Secret and absurd.

You know it happens when no one is looking.
So while he dreamt, you watched for him
talking in his sleep.

The Village Women and the
Swinging Guests (of Tarzan and Jane)

The yodeling man is swinging
through these trees again. His coconut-milk
body slides watery through the sky
like rank old rain.

The smell of him
circles over our heads.
He is a wild thing
who kisses apes
like kinsmen.

He grunts at his woman.
He drags her by the threads
of her hair   when
his nature is high.
Her cry
is the hyena's
out of a giraffe's neck.
She is a delicate thing.
Her cries rise
above the trees
and circle
like scavengers
that threaten us
women as we carry
our water from the river,
    as we beat the ash
        from our clothing.

(It is difficult to be clean
among these swinging guests.
They leave their droppings
all over.)
A court of women
climbed to intercede
in their dispute.
But she turned upon us
    after he lifted
    his fist
    from her mouth.
She spoke from the floor of the tree-
house. From her back.
We left them
to their ape-ways,
those ape-mates.

But, some days when the sky is
quiet, we hear them
rustling through trees,
squandering birds,

disturbing our peace.

Embracing Hansel and Gretel in the
Trickle-Down Time of American Famine

Syringe-thin men with bloody eyes
line up for the empty soup kitchens.

As usual the lies are true:
houses, in famine time, spit out children.
Tables are turned, and stingy
mothers forget birth pangs,
instead nurture hunger
pains. While fathers grind gritty air
between their teeth, wish for a bone to bury
and savor beyond the gnawing
gazes of starving children.

Everyone has a program to run
on an empty stomach:
think of somebody else to sell.
Think of tears boiling in the pot;
they evaporate and steam the bony meat
and stony bread for you alone.

Think of what you want. Listen to your stomach growl.
Worship it.
Think of somebody with a trusting heart
to lead and lose in the forest.
One less mouth to feed.
Think of the food she or he will not use.

We are all children with no more breadcrumbs.
Wandering between thorn-headed trees.
We were hungry. We ate what little we had.
We lost the light. We cannot find our way out.
Our mother is the witch who wants to eat us.
Our father is the one who waits to burn us in his oven.

1984

Mexico City, 1985

for Nora Infante

And then after seven days
the newborn cries inside the rubble,
the cracked shell of earth
and that bright yellow yolk of sound
feeding the dream of miracle.

But the boy, nine, beside the grandfather's body,
died after the heart
tapped out life amid debris
for two weeks, after we had come to believe
what we wanted to believe:

that anyone human can survive catastrophe
no matter how long without what we need.

On Reading Matter

for Denise Levertov

God is a Russian novelist,
                    writing in the snow
            in the loam-earth,
                a long, winding tale
                on reams of flesh.
He typewrites fingerprints,
and footprints,
            He quotes you
            chapter and verse.
This is a good book
and I cannot put it down.
I read it far into the night—
                by starlight
        and moon.
        His terror races hearts.
        Her jokes
            are belly laughs.

God is an African griot;
            a legendsong
                halfsung
            around a sharp, hazy fire
        told only by memory
        told by trance.
I listen to the spell
        binding us and binding.
I join in the singing
and the dance.

God is a poet
        who writes haiku:
    tight, lovely
the images strike
    the eye: sun, bird, mountain
        sea—flood the senses,
    the heart: an inkwell He empties
        and fills.

The Outcast Learns the
Language of Birds

for Denise Levertov and Lorna Dee Cervantes, inspirations

I do not know the names of birds
Hiding in the tall grass
Who rise as one thought
As I pass the slope of the hill.

They talk about me behind my back
Hiding now high in the trees.
They look down on me
Wingless, clumsy, walking.

I am the outcast among the birds.
Though we are all dark and glistening
Before sunset.
They think I cannot speak their language.

But each day the foreigner collects words
Stumbled upon on the hills
Untangled from the sweep of the trees:

They say air,   light,   wing,
Home,   wind,   glide.

Woodside, California, 1983

In Dark Bounty: In Memory of
St. Charles Lwanga Faith Community

for Mrs. Dorothy Mitchell

As high as we were, the church was dark.
And we searched like topsy-turvy magi
for the arrangement of lights below
in the church proper, liturgical for mass at midnight
to break us up before a Christ
painted to look like us whom He resembled at first
                                                    recorded sight.

Willie President, dark-drenched twice,
heavy mouthed, stood toward the high dark,
leaned against the railing, dressed in white
                                        choir robe,
and lifted us in the loft so high
when he opened his thick, sullen mouth and O,
Holy Night came out.

All of this, darkness and lights like tiny dreams,
scattered far below us around the image of a Christ crucified,
and too the cold I remember now warmed over,
lighted up in his tenor, hanging now
when choir loft empties, robes turn yellow as yellowed
milk, and his bones to dust now and forever.

I search high and low for the echo of that holy night,
that sound serene he and we rained down on the service
awed and bent before the birth of God
Who takes this away, and gives it back in dark bounty
                                        beyond touch or sound.

The Resolution

Willie was drinking Mist and mixing batter
and mistook the Mist for milk.
Didn't intend to make so happy a cake
but that was a pleasurable mistake
of which we partook with sliding smiles.
It was too late to turn back
after one and one-half pounds of butter
after a half-dozen eggs devoted to what
was to come in coconut
and chocolate pecan.

This was our lesson for the New Year:

Be devoted to delight, be bringer
of good cheer, stir as right as you
might, and turn away from no
ingenious serendipity, discard no sleight
of hand, and do the sweetest you can.

Faith

Longlegged boys leapt from rooftop to rooftop.
The dark between their legs widening as they spread.

We never questioned the quiet behind the house until the boys made
their legs scissors and cut it. What we thought could not be cut,
as it was made from the stones on the floor of the alley below,
the eaves above the garages that slanted, so standing there was an
art
and lifting off
a greater one.

They could have fallen, but they would not have fallen.
Gifted by heaven to lose gravity in the dark, gain grace
enough to make girls weep to follow, all of us, even looking up,
born anew in midair, no longer grievingly human, mute.
The wind in our mouths. Each breath big, sweetened with amazement.

Once black boys, innocent as angels, leapt from rooftop to rooftop.
Full splits on a floor of dark air, each time a happy ending.
Isn't that enough?

Too Sweet

for my sisters and brothers and their children

This was all so sweet.

Mama opened the door to the White House
her hair disheveled but pinned
her eyes soft with gladness
at the sight of me.
The relief to be so loved so
and welcomed to a kiss
older than I
or she.

All so sweet
when she sent me round
the corner
to get the boy who is my sister's son
my heart stole long ago
for my own.

And the air that night rolling over and over
as delicate   as powerful
as crisp money so much you can only barely imagine it
but cannot conceive
it
not being born
to it.
It was all so sweet.
The gym big and noisy with children
almost women, almost men already grown to the ceiling

dancing from off the wall as the music broke
up to the end of the dance.
And my boy's friend said
he was somewhere
there
in a yellow jacket.

I hunted round and round
through the prosperous squander of children,
older than the music, I
like a berry hunter lost
in a plenty, juicy and staining,
searching for that one.

They spilled out into the street
clustering, bumping against the blue lights
of the police cars.

And the night kept rolling over and over
with bright somersaults of streetlights.

And I could feel my one of few good dresses
swaying around my body
when I walked away
still looking
to the White House.

Sweet
to find that boy I stole
sprawled   exhausted on the couch
after the dance
his girl-cousins falling on his tired legs
tired
he said from dancing
they massaged him devotionally
in that ecstasy of love

lavished by little girls
who are also loved.
And Mama teased some with her daughter's son
"I didn't know you could dance.
Dance for me now."
And the boy who holds the man inside said
"I can't now.
There's no music."
But there was.
There
was.
Rolling over and over
throughout the house,
over the washed wooden floors,
it was.
The music at the dance so loud he said
"You couldn't hear yourself think.
It was so loud
you couldn't hear yourself
talk to yourself."

But it was all so loud, so sweet sweet
in that house
rolling over and over
I could hear myself singing.

I can, even now.

Angelhair

In the redcoat she (who is I) was
an angel, dark and bright.

Mama chose the drama:
pretty scarlet to subdue the white
walk, a world dumb with snow,

patentleather shoes to shine
the path over ice. My

father paid the way.
His teeth salt inside the grin.

I (who's she) had a manner
of leaping toward a light
suddenly running into ecstasy
or heat, exquisitely blind
in the body racing inside it-
self. A little fit of imagining.

Thin arms, cropped wings,
to hold the bristly branches of fir, and sing-
ing, sisters and brothers itching,
happy from angelhair fine as a strand of cat
hair split six ways and brushed into the skin
to itch and itch again.
We were wild and giddy with gifts.

It was then and always as all souls itch and spin
in lit-red coats that float down this narrow vein,
so we spin in O, to someone who loves us

and suffers the world for each turn before a mirror,
quiet as ice, we fall all through at last
here in memory's tiny Paradise.

The Gulf of Blues

On the other end of the line
he sounds like my brother
but is my father
telling me about Coony who is fat.
His whole body like a stomach
round all round, fat even on his head.
Eighty and heavy.
How he joked Coony about his weight,
joking him about a tow truck he'd need
to haul him out of the tub
like an old sunken ship pulled out of
the gulf of blues,
leaving whirlpools in the porcelain.

"Quit all that eating and drinking,"
my daddy say he said to him.
"Quit pointing in that garden and reach down
to get it." My daddy say he joked him,
ribbed him good.
(And I know my daddy laughed gap-toothed,
his mouth, throat, chest, and gut wide
open for the signifying jest.
His gray hair striking back time.)

He sounds like my brother when he was
a little boy, digging in the encyclopedia
for the cause of something obscure, occult,
trying to figure out how old Coony slipped
in the bathtub that was always there

and died like that. Baby Sister called
to tell it first and she wasn't joking
after all like my daddy thought she was,
Death a sad trick children pull.

On the other end of the line
my father sounds like my brother now.
I know how
Dying, bitter or tender, is the dark water that keeps
us young.
And this gulf of blues, deep and shiny,
the only place to be
between Time and Eternity.

Hattie

Your mother outlived you by twelve children.
More's the pity the years spent on the rims
of someone else's jars of jelly or pot of greens.
What sweet or grease could a single woman fall into
with no education, no auspicious skin, and no money
but what she maid for? Only the visits home to Mississippi
—long and industrious—washing everything that would
wash, sweeping, and cooking and eating and gossiping,
done then in lucid harmony to look forward to.
The lovely lace lingerie lay in your drawers
crammed as flowers in Eden, redolent with promise
and sachet. Certain people give what they have
in skinned knuckles and cracking knees please and
thank you.

I keep expecting your just reward for you in this life.
The one you did the best you could by your sister-
dead-before-you's kids. I stick my hand out and
wait for your wages.

"Is this all?" I want to cry like a last-minute virgin,
unsatisfied and raw, as I stand beside the marker
of your small grave life. Grieving the minority
of your simply tendered years. Regretting the tiny
kindness rendered to the huge spirit chastened
in your knuckled-under yet redolent flesh.

Only the air of this fine raiment day kisses my palm
like a lover and a prince.

Caesura

A highschool girl high over the city
riding the el-train (a whip in midair
flung in tempered steel on long black legs)
on the afterschool second wind of adolescence.
The newspaper on a platform,
lines through a window:
Nat King Cole
dead of cancer.
Whatever remark to throw back
at whomever hangs
on the windowed air
like a scribble on sweating glass.
Who, girl, are you to know the sudden fall
of voice to whispers in the vestibule
of the funeral home, the steady fan of dreams
in the old women's hands,
the broken promise of seductive solace
in the sail of song across the dark waters
of the heart's imagination?
O, Imagination, quick slow schoolgirl
riding the flung-out steel
in your promissory sleep,
who are you now to study windows?

The day is punctuated with caesuras,
pauses in the voice, not usually
written down.

Dr. Watts Meets the Man with the White Liver

With appreciation to Ms. Joan McCarty, who recognized the mystery of the man with the white liver and shared her story with me

Dr. Watts

for Joan, Jeff Donaldson, and Phil Cohran at the MBTA in St. Louis, 1984

It is the song every soul knows.
No one knows where it began.
If they did they'd go there when it goes
home.

The throat becomes a cowrie shell
the moan slides through crooked, crowded
with sorrow alive as joy
and joy sounding sorrow sounds.

"Where you from, Dr. Watts?"
say the sister on the mourners' bench.
"Hold my soul, Dr. Watts,"
say the deacon in the amen corner.

Dr. Watts open his black bag
dark as a cola nut,
divinities come rising out.
He got the death rattle in his dark bag.
He got the love cry humming out the womb
and the scrotum.
He got the grave sinking in the soil and the
weeping over it.
He got the waterbag bursting and the birth canal
groaning wide to holler out
arrival.

Back through Middle Passage the Church say amen
and the midnight days of crying
over the tumult water, chaos in the crests,
death in the lowdown leeside of these cruel
mountains of water
in a black canoe of longing sound travels.

Delicate the kiss, nose-touching breathing in, home again
"Where you take me, Dr. Watts?"

"Home again."

"Amen. Amen."

It is the song every soul knows.
It is the song every soul knows
to travel in the hum,
        the groan,
the long way
home.

The Man with the White Liver

for Mrs. Josephine Sankey

He got the thang make a woman cry out in the night.
The man with the white liver
he the killin-love giver.

His first wife die smilin,
say hand me my comb so I can comb
this hair befo that man get home.
His first wife die smilin,
sit up in the sheets
say hand me my comb
before my husband get home
so I can live in his arms
forever. She smilin
reachin and dyin
for the man
with the white liver.
He the killin-love giver.

His second wife die dancin
cross the street dreamin he
standin on the other side
heard him whisperin her name
in the broken car horn
carried her own way from here.
She dancin like Dunham in the middle
of the street dreamin her name on his
sweet, thick mouth, lift her

dress above one knee, raise the
other hand high-swearin she hear her name
in his juicy-dreamy mouth. She
wave to it
and git
hit.
Car with the broken horn
carry her own way from here.
She dreamin about a man
with a white liver. You know him.
He the killin-love giver.

His third wife die like a coffee cup
first thing in the mornin
she dark and laughin when he stirrin her up,
die with a silver spoon in black brew so strong
the spoon stand up
in the cup
first thing in the mornin she die
like maxwell house good to the last drop
people say they read the grinds in her eyes
grinds say lord have mercy I love me my man
with his white liver he the goodest love giver.

He got the thang make a woman cry out in the night.
He got the thang make a woman rise up light as light
and slide through blinds like sunshine.

My girlfriend's mama say tell Angela stay away
from a man with a white liver
    when she find one
    run
say girl stay away from a man with a white liver
he the killin-love giver.
His love take the life

from every smilin wife
he have one behind the other
linin up for lovin
like lambs to the slaughter.
I'm tellin you like I tell my own daughter:
Stay away from a man with a white liver
who make yo liver quiver yo nose open wide
yo heart stop dead in the middle of his rockin ride.

He the killin-love giver.
He got the thang make a woman cry out in the night.
His shoulder the last thing she see.
His coffee cup the last thing she ever be.

Mules and Women

with respect to Zora and the Ground of the African Church

Sorrowtalked eye-to-eye forgiven is no mere burden.
The one who sings is no mere beast.
The one who slips the harness of the horror stands alive
     as earth.

Today I can watch the wind and it is blue smoke.
I shake myself inside my dress, consider rain and choose
     Shine.
I was walking down Mississippi River Street
     and a ghost stopped me.
No one could see it but me,
standing in the middle of the sidewalk
smilin at a haint with his hat in his hand
     instead of his head when he can tote that too.

   When one mule die
   the rest neigh-cry
   till the wagon take the dead thing away.

   Mississippi River Street rampant with noise,
   radiant, won't hold still.
   But I have walked on blue black water.
   Watched dead rise before the wagon came.

   Everywhere I see mules,
   open mouths sing blues, then be human, then
   beyond.

Funerals, weddings, baptisms
I take off my skin, hang it up
like a soaked quilt to dry the tears
and sweat from feeling. I stand naked before Church,
holding Dr. Watts closer than my sagging, girlish breasts.
My soul wears no clothes when she sing.
It is all being in love with more than one
man who is one whole man you can look into his eyes
without blinking.

    Where would I go to hide?
Dr. Watts standing with my skin hooked on his finger
and I am next to him solid and living the song
        with no words
that every born-again mule knew in death and in life
        before
birth, now hums true again hot in the chest and throat
breaking natural out the mouth like breathing.

    Where would I go to hide?
Sit down, rock my soul like my baby and Dr. Watts
climb in my lap and moan for the milk no mother can buy
        or borrow
only make in hearts of her eyes, in lines of the palms
        of her hands.
And where would I find lines with no skin?

    Where would I go to hide?
I tell you I am living now. Like in Mississippi
Grandmama's bedroom sitting on the high bed
        you could break
            your neck leaving.
Cousin Chubby said fried fish, greens, and cornbread was
good eatin. I am good livin. Blue smoke watching,

naked, haint-smiling, entertaining Dr. Watts, dreaming
of a man with a white liver who can't kill me,
who love mulish women, hainted ones,
    I am the sainted one
naked with no sense of memory but good like God rocking
hums in my lap and looking for no hiding place even if
wind be blue smoke hurricane and I make red milk
in the hearts of my eyes and reach out my lifelines to
a hopeless haint I can stand myself.

Naked now, where would I want to go to hide? From this
funeral wedding death and birth baptism
the sliding tears washing my soul cleaner than
Dr. Watts' whistle or the look in a sweatin man's
eyes when he lookin at a perfect, brutal sun
killing him with living while he lick his lips and dream
of water, then put his shoulder behind a woman
guiding him while he dig in and groove the earth
        to the quick
deep endless quick.

    Where would I go
    Where would I go to hide this
    yes-crying love yielding beyond flesh yet
    subsumed by sweat

    Where would I go naked so
    following blues and Dr. Watts
    like a double-seeing shadow
    standing before you with only blue smoke
    between us
    humming yes and yes and yes

    subsumed by sweat and yielding
    beyond mere flesh.

Dark Legs and Silk Kisses

Arachnia: Her Side of the Story

Janet

What Athena weaves best is
lies.   Her and her whole
Olympus family.   Wolfpack of
liars.

She said she was my teacher.
And I swollen imitator, ungrateful
student.
You believe that one?

My body is a busy dark flower
from the dark continent
her Daddy ran-
sacked.   Plundered my pots,
my libraries, my stars, my
gods.

I wasn't from Lydia
either. Wrong girl's name.
I'm the dusky girl from
Memphis.

What Athena weaves best is
lies. Propaganda issued from Olympus.
A thread of deception.
Her stuff sticks to the history
books.
You believe that one?

I wove the real story.
I only embroidered the
                    Truth.
Made it shinier
and it could be seen.
She embroidered seamy press releases
for the Wolfpack
that sits high on the mountain.

She called me blasphemer,
perjurer.   She slapped me
until I spun.   She says she
sent me to the corner and I
hanged my self.
You believe that one?
That she cursed me and would not let
me die?

    It was a lynch-
rope, my Grecian girl wove
for me.
    It was a lynch-
rope, she spun and lay
and waited for me in a
spooky house.

Wolves bayed in the distance
but I didn't listen.
I was busy looking at the sun
god out of a dirty window
weaving his tapestry.
When she fell on me.

It was my murder.
But not my death.

You see this web?

You ever seen anything like it
in this haunted-house world?

I am still working my charms,
                  quietly.

Miz Rosa Rides the Bus

That day in December I sat down
by Miss Muffet of Montgomery.
I was myriad-weary. Feets swole
from sewing seams on a filthy fabric;
tired-sore a pedalin' the rusty Singer;

dingy cotton thread jammed in the eye.
All lifelong I'd slide through century-reams
loathsome with tears. Dreaming my own
silk-self.

It was not like they all say. Miss Liberty Muffet
she didn't
jump at the sight of me.
Not exactly.
They hauled me
away—a thousand kicking legs pinned down.

The rest of me I tell you—a cloud.
Beautiful trouble on the dead December
horizon. Come to sit in judgment.

How many miles as the Jim Crow flies?
Over oceans and some. I rumbled.
They couldn't hold me down. Long.
No.

My feets were tired. My eyes were
sore. My heart was raw from hemming
dirty edges of Miss L. Muffet's garment.
I rode again.

A thousand bloody miles after the Crow flies
that day in December long remembered when I sat down
beside Miss Muffet of Montgomery.
I said—like the joke say—What's in the bowl, Thief?
I said—That's your curse.
I said—This my way.
She slipped her frock, disembarked,
settled in the suburbs, deaf, mute, lewd, and blind.
The bowl she left behind. The empty bowl mine.
The spoiled dress.

Jim Crow dies and ravens come with crumbs.
They say—Eat and be satisfied.
I fast and pray and ride.

Lust: African-American Woman Guild

I wrap my legs around him.
  We swaddle and sway.
     We swing and bring the rain.
      A festival in famine.
      A thunder in heaven.

We curl together. Sex, breath,
and all.   Till I'm breathless.
Quivering.   Complete.

    This is Love.   I sing.
    A tangle you don't mind.
    A hot knot.
    Figure it out.   Anybody.
      Where do he begin and I
        end?

Rock and Roll Monster:
Down Home Blues Goes Hollywood

5527 and the television tribe

She was sitting in her black jook cave
listening to blues, eating bats, and getting fat
when the lightbread people came.
She ate the first man for a snack.

Then the daughter came, with yellow celery down her
back and a boyfriend
and pretty soon a hippy blues spider
can't win.
They took her in,
put her on drugs and propped her in a museum.
Took her blues away.   And she slept,
numb, out of it.
Roped in and stupid.
Captured.
Came alive in a museum in 1957.

Some white kids were playing
rockandroll before the mashed potatoes.
Loud enough to wake the dead or dopey.
Woke the rockandroll in her pitch bush
body. She got up on the wrong side of
no bed. Hair standing all over her head.
Catching radio waves. The Voice of God
she thought it was. She just wanted to
put her hand on the music box and be saved.
Sounded like somebody she knew from home.

But no—indeed—they snatched the
bumpy tune and fled. Scattered down main
street with her musical treat. All she
long for was a good meal after a long sleep.

Evil Gal Blues under her swampy lid.
Crashed
a fine, unshaved leg
through teeny-tiny whitey trim window.
Like a black whip snapping law and order.

Watched the pastel people pee and flee.
Stalked high-heeled blondes with screaming
brussels sprouts in their arms.
All looking good enough to eat, but
rescued in the knick of time.

Monster wanna rockandroll over
in her own bed
back in the jook-joint cave.
She moonlight her Regal walk on home.
Ate
Sheriff intruder at her leisure.
His whole body
hors d'oeuvres.
His skeleton left
an empty lazy susan.

She just wanna pick her teeth, snap
her fingers, drink a bloody mary, and listen
to some down-home blues. Loud.
She wanna lay around with her hair wild
and legs unstyled. Smell her own funk
and dream the rest of her cave-black night.

Got. Instead
a mouth full of dynamite.

Ain't that cold-
blooded?

*The Midnight Market of
Memory and Dream*

grits

all night
she watch the pot, cooked
her grits thick for hours
(not the quick kind) till grains disappear
into smooth with a slick

coat on top
hot enough
for a man to wear
(she said) on both
his faces.

greens

this is the kind of love you write home about
in sunlight the single aunt sits round
the harsh wood table and sighs. you know how

strong the smell of mustard greens is.
and bitter the turnip. spinach,
on the other hand, goes down easy.

all this cooking in her one pot when
you write home the kind of love
it is.

in an african light

the sun a sauce in the skin
oil
in the coiledgrains of the hair

the sun a sauce
honeys
yam over bone and burning

condiment
of woman
a light musk of spice for the sauteed/wind
with breasts swinging
heavy as the swelling
brown
beans

brandy-eyed
brother:shadowing

connoisseurs
of african cuisine

Wares for the Man Wherever
This Song Is

I sell the songs
that sailed the summers
    of
        stockingcap & afro pick
I lay the story
     on black
     wax
   with a wish
   memory tugs

   in its physical way
   an infant pull
   at the breast, the nipple,

   chipped & mouthed
   womb draws
   to a close & fans
   herself from the inside

enter the hero, smokey throat/d
on the spotlight stage of my voice

   a body easy
   a black
   finger long rhythm
   touching along the rhythm-root
rhythmic
   until I can lay
   back into a beg

        barely above the air
        absolute and fragile
        lips parted full of song
        trying to hold on not fall
        between my own limbs
        or fly

where he works with a horn
touching four corners of the room
spreading blue
light and tension, yes I

want to do the slow drag and african twist.

Hootchie Cootchie Man

for Billy Branch and the Sons of the Blues

I think of you
Hootchie Cootchie Man
in the seventh season
in the seventh second
of the seventh minute
of this seventh song
when the room
turn blue
fire-eating indigo
and azure sure
flickers from
a guitar-man fingers.
I think of you
the harmonica man
eyes unfocused
centered on the inside
where music rules

eyes closed
I see you
where music breaks
the concrete of my
poise, and indigo
flower flames between
the wrapped legs
of my heart—
the one you broke

with a black cat bone.
I sucked on bad luck
and saved my soul
the only way I could.
Blues.

This is the way we worship
here.
I can shake
my head and shuffle
from wide hips,
pucker my mouth
for the shimmy-kiss of
air.
Hootchie Cootchie Man
if I join you here
juke-jointed and humming
healed
we make a peace
with time
and old crime—
mockingbird move away
this man is here
to stay
amid all
mint julep misery
and sloped city
slew-footed loneliness,
one-eyed pride
we razor at the throat.
Hootchie Cootchie Man

I got a song and a stance for you.
I got a victory dance for you
a blackberry sweetness

wearing a red dress
and shaking it,
shaking it
in yo blue, laughing
sweat-dipped face.

Mr. Snake, I Don't Like You

I don't like you today, finally
and forever.
Before, there was always something
about you
to claim for amazement and goodness.

I always assumed your injury.
Because you did not fly I told people
you were mending a broken wing.
The truth is you cannot fly.
Some terror in you keeps you hugging
the ground.

Like a snake's your eyes are always open
guarding your poisons.
You imagine thieves who want to steal
your skin. You nightmare with open
eyes. The day is cool, peaceful, and
I walk with nothing to harm you.

I do not want to take you home, Sir.
You are best left in the wild tasting
your full stomach.
I only wish to watch, to tell people,
our mutual acquaintances, about the
patterns of your skin.

The truth is you swallowed the bird inside
you, so all of you is snake.
Eternally serpent.

They have come to tell me of your hard,
open eyes. What crimes you imagine of me:
Lucretia, Lizzie, Lady
Macbeth.

Mr. Snake in your Snakedom, what
fantastic dreams you weave.
We are not all made of your skin.
We are not all snakes.
We do not all lie with poisons.

Only the ones who close their eyes
to dream
can rise.

Doubting Thomas

Doubting Thomas reached into Jesus
and found the flesh to stop his own

Hand-jive. He had the nerve
    to be surprised.

He marveled at the triumph: blood
& bone infused

    by Holy Ghost.

In catechism they said—
    the spirit came to visit
    the body the host.

As if the house
    built the house
    and lived in it.

Dear Thomas, forehead creased like
    the fold in a sleeping
    sparrow's wing:

The first, the cause of triumph
    is birth.
The spirit seen fit
    to dabble
    in matter, when it will
    or please, every now
    and then.

Do we make too much of a short-term
    lease?

Monroe, Louisiana

for Gwendolyn Harvey

in the northern morning
two hundred children weeping thru candleleaves, a swamp
of bird cries muffled in woolen memory, the voicesong of his
rising on a cool and beautiful blade, going thru us

we walked down the aisles holding flat our severed, wild
pain, moving in circles like ghosts from eyes,
not wanting to touch each other, to set too much in motion

in the southern evening
we watched the wounded cotton in a fenced field, none of us
could believe beyond

he had a name we had never heard before
in full
spoken in voices brownsuited with love

we swallowed his life whole: counted the flowers and blood
sunlight falling thru half-open curtains

everything he had touched we
touched, went inside
his mother

till she spread her arms
in the church and
flew
her burly brothers
holding her to the
earth

his house was a world
of embraces, and tangible
air: we were holding him, his brothers and sisters, he
was holding us

only his arms are wider than his mother's
the night she flew

On the Train that Glides from
Plane to Plane

Homeboys: Dip and Sid

each of you was ending your journey
when i was somewhere between my life
you were climbing down from the
hissing train, jaunty, young, strong-faced,
slinging your heavy baggage careless as
you walked with startled grace just ahead of the wind
our wide eyes
latched onto you with your marvel
and quick flair cornering you in the moment
you were climbing down from that train that
shuddered like a heart that cannot decide whether it
is dying or loving
climbing down jaunty with the heavy baggage
walking one-sided and brave aside the cold smoke
of the shuddering train
how far
and where am where am I on the track only settling
down for the journey with a shoebox lunch of almost
memories for a brief life? some where mid-way? crawling
through a tunnel
crying without sound? or
climbing, climbing
down
to meet you?

another time, the forms of famine

another time
women questioned with leaf-light
coffins

men sat toothless on their
haunches, legs ashen
riddled with waste

no different the women wailing over
bones
no different this commercial street coughing
thru the windows
of gutted buildings
boys with attitudes they cannot spell circles
in the square
the man leaking curses on the woman's
face for our eyes to latch upon

this time, going home, to lights or no
lights
we answer each other's breathing in the end-
less dark,
scratching for roots to settle our hungers

The Cost of Living

is far
too high
life will split you along your back
like the fisherman's wife who tears
the blackspine from the
shrimp
for her gumbo

at the corner market of men
she shops:
a lb. of flesh
& blood & brain
matter she feels
her scarred vegetables

if i should find you
so
refused
in a midnight market of memory
that runs the length of the el
where voices are made of train
wheels
moving
and your name is not spoken

i would find you curled and crusted
waiting to board
yet
where layers of flesh have fallen from you

and wrinkled the earth to madness we
would fall into place: bowled-seats

would cut out each others' eyes and stare
against the glass-peeling
where our names are not spoken

i will say that i saved you from
                    pity
you will close your spine's space
where
the strength has been torn

the cost of living
        is far too
        high

the heart cannot afford
        such expensive feasts

Practicing Patience

Jonathan Smith

Think of country roads, dusk and dust.
Think of rivers, flat or wild.
Think of moonlight.
Things that last forever.

Think of quilting.
Think of washing greens.
Think of cleaning chitterlings
    with your face turned away
    wrinkled up in eager disgust.
    Scrape the stink from the lining.
    Scrape and pray the stink away.
Think of the curves on the rocking
chair.
Extend.
It is a circle.

Walk winding like a road.
Walk like a river.
Walk like moonlight.
Walk however long you need for dust to
    settle within you.
Walk forever.

Quilt. Wash greens one leaf at a time.
Clean chitterlings, if you must. Scrape
inside the wrinkle of things.

Sit and rock to the edge of the runner.
Extend. You are a circle.

Remembering

Remember, the blurry sun you could not
    see. Heavy, huge, hungry
    inside of you.
Remember, the air that turned to
flesh, the flash, the sweat
    ravenous for you
    in you.
    Lightning
inside you.
      The swollen fruit
      that fainted but did not
      fall. Hung, huge.
      Oh, the heavy blue sky.
      Oh, the arms
      around you
      like a feast of dreams
      and good, good fortune
      and rescue
      and sweet religion.
      Each moment
      a pomegranate seed.
      A thousand
      in the mouth.

      Do not spit them out.

      Oh, recall the Time
      Love walked like thunder
      through you,

and its footsteps made
prints in you
no wave,
no sea of harshened sorrow
can obliterate.

Remember the sun
ravenous for touches, delight.
And the hot, hot rain
that fell and opened
bruised petals
in a thousand red flowers:
All of them some part of you.

The Bloom Amid Alabaster Still

for Eli Smith at Lifeline

the living image of god
walked amid alabaster
a thin dark bloom

pierced
earlobes
and outlined
eyes

a comely woman she has a son for us who know him now
a nubian beauty near nightmare and morning

one ear, pierced a-
glittering
and outraged
eyes

the living image of god
a full dark bloom
from a blue lotus

give him now this son a gift to wade golden
a journey under the viaduct of nightmare and mourning

and his name be strange to dying
and singing now strange to dying

The God of Fire

The God of Fire

I am the little girl who plays with the god of fire.

He bites my lips
          and scars my hands.

"Little girl." He tells me.
"Don't you know I'd run through you
          like a silver knife?
Burn down all your trembling houses?"

"Yes." I tell him.
"I have watched you a long long time without
winking.

          I know the cruelty
          of your ember.
          I have read your mark on women's eyes."

I touch him without squinting.
He bites my lips and scars my hands.

Full height
he draws himself up.
          He is one flame that flares
red and blue against the trees.
          Lightning.
          Over the sand.
             Over the houses.

"Listen, when I tell you
          I am fire, little girl.

I am son
and father of the sun.
I will make you ash and curling smoke."

"I know," I whisper into the deep blue flame.
My lips are red with him.

"God of fire who burns
poison out of wounds.
Son of fire who
bites the ice
        and makes it sweet.

Father of fire
who
watches the earth.

You are a god of mercy.
Have mercy on me.
Be tender with my meat."

I look into his light
        and wink.

"Little girl," he says. "Who owns you?
                Where is your home?"

"I am only a child.
        Water.
        Early to bed.
        River
    of invisible rises.
    The beautiful daughter of many people.

I strike fire back at the sun
            and it is glass.
Have you never seen the water that
            holds the fire?
                Cradles it
            and rocks it
            into weaving smoke?
You must have something soft against you.
You are more child than I.
You are thirsty.
And will burn yourself out."

"No," he snaps and hisses.
He is full of caprice.

He bites my lips and scars my hands.
Curses me with thunder.

I am too still,
            without a murmur.

He is wary.
A muscle of contempt.

We watch each other.
And we wait.

The Autumn Men

in autumns what i remember is
my father and uncles gathering buckets
and rakes doing the earth's duty
with a calm and ritual therapy they
worked the wrinkled, sunset leaves
into mountains
like a sacrifice of lovely and faded women
the men gave leaves to fire

the smoke would rise
                       black and full of husky

sexual smell
the men would lean on their rakes and watch
their children would flutter and swirl around the smoke and
bodies

my father would gather the ashes into buckets and discard them

now this daughter is fallen,
sunsets, and gathering her body for
giving

it is a new time, for life
and fire must be fed

A Woman Along the Way

An amber woman ambles in her garden of frozen fruits and vegetables.
She calls to me, in her hands tomatoes and okra, her voice full of
admonitions:

> I was one entranced, violated by flame.
> I stared too long into the roar.
> Music
> took my hands. I circled myself in wild paint and
>   watched my body move into heat.

> I was hungry all the time. Fire was delicious:
> an inflammatory statement.
> You know he was.
> I loved his devastation, continuing combustion.
> I indulged him too much. He raged unchecked, petulant,
> spoiled.
> I swear. His language was abusive. His expressions cruel
> grimace and scowls.

> Let me give you a caution: give him only the animal
> exchange of energy. He does not know the sacrament
> of the heart. His is a bleeding ulcer.

> But who am I to say a thing or two? I have grown old.
> I have a loose mouth. Once my cheeks were round and fire
> swelled inside me until I burst.

My eyes glisten in genuine distress. Questions levitate and fall.

And then I said, "No one tells the same story twice. Tell it to me
again."

What she said is this:

>Woman is a language of no more than tree:
>he roots.
>he branches.
>he breaks.
>he leaves.

I sucked my teeth at her old wives' tale. "How he leave after he
breaks? Nothing leaves after it's broken," I insisted.

Her eyes wandered and her voice wrapped round me like a vine,
an ivy, holding me:

>What is man will lay you waste.
>Gods such as they are.
>Will open you, rotate a crop of jubilee
>and suicide, then will lay you waste, will lay you waste.
>   Am I right
>or wrong?

Litany

With palms
I shielded my eyes
from possible pain.

I gathered my courage, cleverness, and voice
   spoke
   his litany

My face in the earth beneath his feet.

"You were a god before music
       fell and broke into voices
       before
the tribes were marked limb
     from limb, eye
     from eye, skin
     from skin, heart
     from heart, and
     brain
       before
desire was formed out of hormone, mucus, and marrow

before Osiris
You were a god

before the market of salt, and spices and trade
beads
before rice rose out of mud

before bruteforce
You were a god before the deathhowl

before The Chain
before The Coffle

You were born before hallelujah, as old as hosanna!
before the plain and orangebreasted lizard made marriage patterns
in the sand
before the funeral of justice, before mercy
before '27, the flood, when the house was torn from its roots
and twins were birthed on the roof. before the river ran wild
before the anger of water. before the beacon, and the light-
house

You were a being before the Hawk and The Holy Ghost danced
as one on the corner of Celebration
and Sanctuary, before the women of the creme sachet and
toilet water lay
with porcelain gods and works
of art.
You were there in The Time
        of the North Star
        in The Time
        of the Moss that hugs the Tree
        of Memory
You are as old as the longing for Messiah
Your lifeline equatorial and your heart
bleeds back from the long tunnel of The First God
You have accumulated more pain than I.
I have heard of you.
I know that I am young."

"Magician of two thousand smoke screens.
Griot of light years,"
then I raised my face to his, to meet him
        an eye for an eye.

"People say I am aglow, a star
has set upon me.
        And I am patient
        as the moon."

"You are a fool," he said.
"Beyond a shadow," I replied.
"I am ready for giving. I have come singing.
I know that I am young."

Cayenne

I prepared a lamb for him (a sacrifice floating
        in herbs and
        blood and water)
        seasoned with salt of
            camouflaged tears
      onions
        and three kinds of
      peppers
        enough
        to kill
        a goat.

My mouth shaped half a plate of triumph.
I held murder in my hands.

He sat on his throne, a luxuriating storm.
His neck was stiff
as an eagle's.
He watched the sway
of my hips,
      heavy, widened
      as I walked
      with design.

He took the dish
and tasted it.
      He ground West African pepper with his teeth.
        He lulled his tongue inside the heat.

Then
he said, "This is not sweet enough.
There is not enough salt."

He crushed my eyes
for salt.
He opened my veins
for syrup
and let my laughter over
lamb.
Devoured it. (His teeth cracked bone.)
Devoured it. (He sucked the marrow.)

Then
he roared
for more.

I gave him my mouth.
He pulled my kisses till I
was gaunt. My joints grew thin
as spider tapestries.

Still, he said he was not satisfied.

I fell behind my mask
inscrutable
wall of
water
silent hieroglyphic
of hurt.

Reflecting,
I watched his fine teeth
glisten
while he laughed.

Fire Is Absolute

Fire is absolute.
You were absolutely right.

I should have known
       I had no ways
              I had no means enough

       to know. I, who have always
              been water.
Fire burns.

              Grates the eyes
              Peels
              flesh and sears

Fire:
you are absolute.
There is no defense.   A woman who loves fire
              who meddles with flame
              who flirts with tongues
              will
              burn
              will
              be

              consumed.

In the village, on the street corners
the women
raised their skirts
and only fanned the flame. Fire rose around their thighs.

Went through them
and blossomed between their breasts.

Fire licked their ankles and they danced.

Fire:
you are music   nobody has business
                          listening to
                          alone.

(And when I touched you you were warm. I cupped the heat
and laughed into the colored shadows you cast across my skin.)

I was laughing, people say,
not like a little girl.
They say I raised my skirts delicately,

like a lady, and danced

till they only saw   the smoke.

So This Is How the Women

So this is how the women
gods lost divinity or

so you say
they
lay down in still spinning silk beneath
the brass sound of his

flesh

fortified in movement
and desire, flashing

till the voices of angels
eluded them

and they were only earth and water
looking at the sky.

Solo in the Boxcar Third Floor E

Solo in the Boxcar Third Floor E

           The single
I, as woman, have never discarded
my house like a snake
and taken up new fixtures, furnitures
never have I before this   torn up tables

rooted to one spot in the floor, dragged
out the couch to hang over the back banister
or lain down broken on a sweating man's flannel back

standing in the backyard with its guts
hanging out
the dresser indecent without drawers
                        out of place

too heavy for me suddenly   sunflower fragile

boxes of dreams unborn going down three winding stairwells
on a working man's
                whistle

I sway thru the window of this
                        just
                        hanging curtains
                        with sun intricate in my full eyes

Listening to women below talking about what
men are good for
                and where:

           traveling between planes
           who carries
           the baggage, thru customs?

who, stripped beyond waist and glistening,
loads the freight

of feminine flesh
trembling to slide thru midnight
train whistles?

Mr. Solomon and His Queen

After he teaches her
   who he is
   and how a woman sup-
   pose to be.
After he learns her good.
   He puts her out
      the house
in her slip—you know the one—
black as sloe,
and the limpstrap that dips
over her shoulder onto
the arm—that one.

After he listens to her
     in the hall
   through
   the wailing wall
   the China-high wall long
   between them—
He lets her back in . . .
   to get her coat.

After he ignores her, they breathe brokenglass air,
          and divided dreams.

After he lets her go in peace—
    he plays his rumbling blues
    loud—about tumbledown love, loss of
        pride,
        callused work, and shotglass, gutbucket
        time,
        open-fly, loose-boweled feeling,
        all night long
        till daylight
sensible sun
    come creeping home
    and she does too . . .
            dress on, coat on arm, over
                shiny gun in hand. "Hit me
again,
            and I'll use it."

.

Woman in Moonlight Washes Blues from Dreams

I do not believe God made me as less.
Or that the presence of a secret mouth
silences the seen.

I do not fear service
in the ritual, Creation.
On the seventh day of love
I bowl clean water in my palms
swing a clean towel across my shoulder
to wash where God has joined Himself
to Herself.

This business, afterwork, makes me more.
Reaffirms the cleanliness of all joy.
(In the moonwatch I have loved you
    even after Loving.

You were still and tired of the tide.
Washing.)

Silence. I do not fear
Silence. Lying plain on any lips.

I do not fear moonwork or sun,
Silence
or music of mouths.

In the dark only love lurked to leap out
at me. Like light on my feet, jingling
like strings of beads
adorning

my nakedness
as I moved from Cleansing to
cleansing.

You, there in her bed,
What monsters breathe over your shoulder
as you turn to face the wall
and sleep?

Festival

you have heard
the impassioned question
of pacifists:
what if they gave a war
and nobody
came?

this query's distressed
a-whisper
inverted and the same:
what if you gave
a love
and nobody came?

The Witherspoons:
Walk Up, Bell Out of Order

As a witness I can speak for both parties. I can speak for her
I can speak for him, mumbling like he does through a gold
toothed grin, and sheepish eyes.

Really she did
and she does

love him more than the words
she sent tangled after him through the door
way
curses on the wind
out the window

his clothes
cut puzzle pieces and sailing
after she scissored them
with a rage, the striped gray businessman's suit and the devil
ish scarlet surprise jacket in velvet he loved to touch
when nobody saw

she loved him knife-deep worse than a glancing blow
love went thru her
sharper than
the razor she wrote with

shone brighter
than the lamp always winking she broke
on his back, it was lovely, beige and brass-based, either very
antique or very cheap.

She did too and she does love him.

I tell you.

She tell him.

Late at night I would hear them, after the storm blew over
leaving its tucked tail of silence.

He says, "Baby,
    what I'm gonna do
    with you?"

"Just keep on loving me." She says.

"Just
keep on loving me, Honey."

The Mother Behaves Like a Young Woman with a Lover when Nat King Cole Comes on the Box

She takes off her run-over shoes.
She removes her re-run stockings.
She unzips her re-hemmed skirt.
She parts with her polyester blouse.
She lies down on the sagging couch.
Husband and children hide in the living room dark.
The television glow slides over her slip
Like moonlight.
Nat King Cole's glossed hair glistens like an onyx.
His voice shines in her eyes. She closes them.
His song ends on the edges of her
Mona Lisa smile.

Midnight sighs over the silence of sleeping children.
She sleeps on and on the sagging couch.
Until husband invites her to his bed,

His voice
    newly tender,
    newly televised.

Black Atlanta Mother Waits at Window, 1981

Strange.
The Silence of this nation is not strange.
    The President does not speak to me.
        A son breaks
        easy as a flower.
            (Lynched pistils, nectar
            spilled.)
Where I step
tears fall, turn to
crystal at my feet,
shiny like beads on a
President's lady's shoes.

Strange. No one
cries with me but
the ones who are me. Fields
who understand the
    quiet of slaughter.
    Remember all my sons,
    my one or two
    daughters. Remember
Devastation
of a field of flowers.
    The President is on tv.
    His only words are: stop
    inflation (running away on blood-
    beaded slippers).
No one speaks to me.
On the absence of simple flowers
in this house-
hold.

The Brother Guild Calls the
Game on Sunday Afternoon

When the weather is fine
        like a good woman
    who can cook, laugh, love, and be
    quiet,
    the Brother Guild meets
        on the second floor
behind the blues door,
        choric discords
        break out the window
            antiphons
            to the sports-
            caster priest.

    Free as a runaway
laughter crashes
    through
    in bounty broad daylight
    —such audacity
—such vicarious
Victory.

They lean back after dinner
     and smoke it like a good cigar—
     rolled between fingertips,
          sniffed,
               nibbled at the end (one bit stays on the tip
                    of the tongue),
          lit,
          drawn, lingering,

     in the mouth;
     in the air
          a hubris-halo,
          heroic aura,
     a smooth, melodic aroma

     like the richmen
     wear.

Loving

David and Vivian

It is
like/ making a cake.
The butter must yield/
easy to the spoon, and the
fall of sugar
The eggs/ warm yolks
spread like sunsets
   in the bowl/
   Salt pinch/ flour pound/ baking
powder be sifted/
shaken down/
It is/ like
making a cake
   baked
in the right container
at the
right temperature

It all/ has to be
   there.

Woman Pitting Fruit at the Kitchen Window

What part of me, seeded, nurtured the
bad fruit, the love?

Was it the crowsfeet
folding my eyes, fearing, resenting
   my own last blossoming?

     The spoiled baby?
     The lost child begging embrace?
     The bookish one experimenting
     with touch?

What part fed the devil-need?

     My nose African flat,
     small pecan eyes, or large
     lipped mouth?

     Was it my hips, sealed lush, or breast
     swollen with months, unmouthed?

What error in me, mismade and hungry,
        did this?

What perfect charity?

Miz Sheba Williams: As Told to This Reporter from the Community News Front

I used to live by the window
barely lifting the blinds
after Mr. Williams died
and our children grown
moved away from home
and up around where the white
folks stay.
I could bend my elbows
in my kitchen at last
stretch my legs in bed.
Plenty of room to breathe
on my own.
But even my throat closed up.

There was murder outside my door.
And no use for age.
Too many twisted in a twisting
rage
or praying they way into designer
jeans
so they can wear somebody else's
name on they behind.
A brand name.
My mama told me enough
about the days of wearing
somebody else's name.

I stayed behind my blinds,
so nobody could see up in here
my 19 inch screen tv my daughter brought
me
my stereo my son say now I can hear
Amazing Grace. The instrument
so sensitive, so sensitive you can
hear a angel clear her throat
in the background while Aretha
lead the seraphim and cherubim
on through it.

Row by row
they lined up below my window.
Smoking them funny cigarettes
or just plain ole Kools.
They talk a lot about the weather
(freezing in it), about war (dying
in it), about women (getting in it),
about money (grabbing holt it).
How would I know ever which one of them
stole my Social Security check?

Not that nice one who carry my grocery
bags, and pick me up off the ice
and tote me home
and call my children
and the ambulance didn't come for a long
time.
After all that, he wouldn't take a thank
you dime from me.

He remind me of someone.
No. I would not go
to live in children's homes.

I couldn't leave Mr. Williams' memory
alone.

He was the one made me open my window
and holler down at him one shiny day.
I say, "Come on up here and taste
these greens. Put some pep in yo
step. I mean."
Here he come in my doorway.
Looking like Mr. Williams, my own.
He seventeen, smart and lean.
I'm eighty. He call me lady.
I pray I die long before he do.
And he use what I give him
in my aged days.
He beg for my secrets. "Miz Williams,
why you wanna take yo knowledge
and hide?

I used to live by the window.
Now I live outside.

That ain't such a big story, darlin',
but believe you me,
it's history.

PoemMaker

for OBAC

in the marketplace
they sell scandal and heartbreak
tomorrow's antique
bracelets of an ancestor's teeth

all my goods are marked
"Made Inside" under the heart
and immaculate eyes
I do not translate into cash
money: confetti and brass
ready for ware
and made to order, not my own

me?
I do not sell
well

Who Would Trade It? Who?

DFaye

who would trade

those days
sucking on the gold tooth
delicious
the black
iron   /pot
                    liquor
of it
the gumbo hours
above the flame
            given
            the swagger for hips
            and sweet for lips
to shake out the empty mattress
over the back
                    balcony railing
with blue reeling
around the flat air

who would trade beads of rose, revelations,
                    and sultry
                        religion
the warm arm span, and wide of hand
to shake out the empty mattress
over the back

        balcony railing
with blue reeling
around the flat air

after love has raised the lilac, and maroon blossomed
money of the trees, after i got down royal in the streets

like a rich fool woman

Making the Name

Call me, call me, call me, call me, baby.
—Aretha Franklin

name me a woman who can get so
drunk
    half a cup of syllables, first thing

    in the morning, late at
    night when the moon winks wicked
    while I essay poetically past with my shoes in my hand
    foolish on the curb of your voice
    walking in my big feet and palm legs
all of me
fondled in the palm
wine
of your language, changed plain
water to wine, burnished
a brandy to slide
so
easy down
among all the jive and solemn verbs

call me she who
      is
      made word
inebriated, inebriant
    all done up and delicious

so I could stay out later than moonlight &
sneak in the backdoor of a wedding night with
    a giggle in my throat

    walking soft
in my bare feet and silk
    woven legs
in soot hair & eyes, a stream
of ssshes parting my lips, I would not
wake the war in you

beloved

        I am the name of peace,
        and drunken victory,
    the luscious part-
    ing of speech

Song of the Writer Woman

Husband
These poems are your rival.
   They undress me.
   They keep me up nights.
      Turn my eyes to soft fruits
      ripe and realized.

Husband
These poems are my best friend.
   They listen to my monotony,
   my unceasing repeating.
   Against their patience I
   can never sin.

Husband
These poems are my passionate suitor.
   They go down on one knee.
   They beg me, "Marry me. Marry me."
   I find
   I give them my hand.

Husband
This could be exciting: poems&me, you&me,
Ménage à trois. Permanently,
Happily.

Husband
Is a woman poet permitted bigamy?
Husband
Answer me!

Sojourner: Traveling Light

because of Sterling Brown
for Melvin, for Soyini,
for Sojourner, the music women

Those traveling men swooping onto
        freight cars
   like
   birds too big
   for backporch
       rails
   too great for crumbs
from window box
   women
   with open palms,
are not all gone
       in history.

But in wind
       swooping and leaving
       droppings
          in women's palms.
Traveling, in Black folk
lore, is a man's thing.

A rolling stone gathers no moss, ties,
no memory.
He looks to the North Star
with a blues under his belt.
Future in his footprints, random,

defiant. Train whistle,
a lure, a fishing line that curves
through the open window of his eye,
pulls his life
out of his wife's arms.
Her throat desert.

A boybaby tosses covers
from tiny itching feet.
The women cry, "Born
to ramble." A piece of
North Star in his eye.
A wordless holler
under his belly button
a quarter tied to it, pressing down
seven seas in his soul. Rocking.

*

Lot's wife didn't know how to get hat
and go.
She had to look back.
She had to season leaving with too much
salt.
She had to fill the pot
till it was too heavy
to carry.

*

I have broken myself carrying
a house of memory on my back
like a dumb turtle, thirsting.
Then, fallen, watched sorrow
tumble into the road, milk and
eggs spilled, old teeth chipped,

blues blurred into dust.
I have broken myself traveling
heavy lumbering while birds
spun over me, and whistles
wrapped my wrists and would not
let me stop. Would not.
All was lost.
And nothing.
Now.
This sweet, original day I set out,
milk wiped, and egg,
my face,
restored.
Let me travel light, following
footprints I only dreamed.
A woman in an early blues I say,
I'll "pack my grip and make my
getaway."
Now I am led by a thread of moonlight
and more, offering peace.
Crossing over the ocean
of air.
Now I am Janey's daughter—
horizon curled in her lap like a content cat
I stroke and hold, the calico sun.
Now I am Harriet-hero, Moses-
woman, deliverer of lost,
traveler,
Sojourner who took up new name, new tract,
and does not look back.

*

Traveling, they say,
is a man's thing.

I rode a nightmare to get to this.
How would they know the tracks I dreamed?
I bled out ovaries and made blueprints.
Wept-hearted I could not sleep
while boxcars of disappointment
rumbled in a wet night.
The noise drilling through my eyes.
Bursting.

In the morning, years later I was alive.

This is what the distances sing.
The many distances wept clean
The many distances swept clean

Wait for me under maps of moonlight,
austere and serene.
Anytime you love, do it with an open hand.
I am a traveling woman. Memory safe in a window
box of wherever I do not remove from, even while
riding a midnight. Loving this.
Mossy-dipping in the deep blue air-well,
leaving light,
O, traveling, traveling,
traveling light.

Rain

It was raining war
so they went to the hills
the ones they blessed
in the many names of God
of Ibadan.
They ate only pigeons,
snails, and wild mango.

It is raining love
or something.
I journey into the hills
the ones you blessed
and drank from
my breasts   you said
the many names of God.
I eat only milk,
fire, and wild eggs
from birds
who adore their own wings.

Woman Watches Ocean on a Reef through a Glass-Bottomed Boat

In the ocean one fish
swallows the other:
a geometric progression of
loss.
You are bigger than I.
The calamity of love
swelling out larger than us.
And what destiny partakes of
our dilemma?
Swallows the cause and effect:
eyes and kissing mouths and enlarged
parts wanting to breathe and wanting.

There is no gentle sense to this.
Is there?
Only a kind of terror
at the chain
of events, the scale of loss, the ordered

destruction one against the other—
all that something larger
awaits its moment.

Conversation with Catalpa Tree

Gwen and Nora

For as long as you are, I remember.
Counsel me with your height. Let me laugh broad
leaves like you. Generous tree, giving away cigars
like a father whose baby has been born.
Celebrating birth.

You were the first tree I noticed
as a child. You made yourself known, a flamboyant spread
across the gangway. Leaving leaves and cigars the mannish boys
retrieved to smoke till they were stomach-sick of your
potent magic.

Your leaves I dreamed were
ships I floated across the sea that came after rain.
One leaf was turtleback, or plate
to balance on my knees.
Whatever I dreamed.

I know you. You harbor in your arcs
some quests of a girl
who became
me.

You give her back to me
in your leaves,
broad like my laugh

in your cigars
potent like my magic

in your branches
embracing like my arms.

A House of Extended Families

Kinsmen: An Address

I am your mother.
I must tell you
to protect yourself
against women who think of you
as a Thing. A simple, muscular corpus
genuflecting to their whims.
A Black Devil with a pitch
fork they would sell their souls
for and
you your mother's beauty.

Must I remind you?
I am your mother.

There are women who can take
a divining stick
and find water anywhere it hides.
I can take this Black hand
or only the divining end of a
finger
and ease over you all over and
be tender at each place you are
vulnerable.

I live in the land where you live.
I would not exploit your resources
or your failures.

Need I bind you to me?
I am your kinswoman.

What
fevers you have
I have.

        What immunities you need
I give you:
            transfusions, donations
      of organs.
See this skin
for grafting?
      We are compatible.
         You and I.

Your first food swells and sweetens
         in my breasts.
     I do not beg
       to nourish you.

greenville

mouth/greasy
and diaper/wet
me   in a oldmans thin thin arms
   wrinkledwarm&
   brown
   full of granpapas food&fussin
   bout them kids
   leavin this here littlebaby
   by herself
and my brothersandsisters
skippin down the road like
duststorms skippin like

dizzy dazzlestones across the water

i couldn't catch up with

john jackson

grandaddy
your pears were hard
green granite
yet
you guarded them from
bird and child (the pecking
order)

each after
noon your young
woman would come to wait
on you and
what did she get
for it?
in your garden of pears and pecans
i
pushed the swing that held
one of over fifty
all
of us toughened
by your quartered dreams

home trainin

my father never did
heal my smart talkin
mouth. no matter
how many pursuits

around and under the kitchen table
with belt or extension cord.

i had two smartin legs
        (and ass)

but my mouth
        continued to sass.

The Robinsons

circa 1925 or 30

sidney, sitting
suited for anything
fingers crossed
around his cigar like a thorn
and legs crossed over
his luck.

alcie's eyes huge
and dark
with marriage
and three red children.

all got up
and dreaming.

early evenings

early evenings and the streetlights
not yet on
we carry/d the backyard
to the front
cement
and study/d the street
while jumping double dutch
or irish in case of tie
waiting for the seven fifteen
bus
bearing our mama

bus rush by kicking dust and paper
and us all raggedy
me—a rather wild child
racing to the corner

mama would wait out a light
and rest
       her shoppingbag
we would rip it from her and
worry
it
for a surprise
empty or not
       there was a happiness:
the gift of her
brownred/yellow and laughing
           weariness
rests easy in our eyes . . .

other evenings

other evenings when we called
ourselves ladies
of leisure
too cute for doing dishes and
washing and sweeping and cooking
chores like our mama did for life
being too much women
grown and fine we decorated
the streets
flirted and jived
till the sun blinked a warning
about work to be done
before the old girl
arrived.

aunt beebee

no obscene odor.
no smell of tainted meat. no
remembrance ravages the nostrils.
nothing telling dying
but her arms. her thin thin thin arms

stretching to em/brace me to
brace this child against the shock
of her loss.
her eyes of worn tenderness . . .
her bones barely cloaked in comfort given . . .

i hold her gentle gentle pity.
o lord. i got her hugging me.
knowing.
she was the living/one.

in my father's garden

anyway and how

my mother does work in my father's garden.

this afternoon without wind
                of september in heat

the monkeycigartree once struck by lightning
grows anyway and how

its roots have begun again to be
                         at an awkwardheight
and this afternoon of lazysun   bloomed in heat

the tree bends and touches the greens
and squash in my father's garden begun from brick and rocks

we thought
                 the only thing that would grow in this city
                 would be brokenglass
on vacantlot and faithshoveled
my father planted anyway and how.

he set this task, and grew his greens too close
like people in tenementrooms.
                   and my cousin fixed the seeds
                             that opened crampedyellow
              transplanted them in sun and soil and air.
              her hands are whiskey and kindness. like
              herself.

my father's garden grew.
he never knew my cousin's sharing. her healingcare.

now. ready for evening my mother does work in
my father's garden.

the monkeycigartree my brothers smoked stalkthings that grew
from it pumped magic in their heads   once
grows again and bends and touches the greens the squash the beans

and my mother bends and touches like treeshadow her orangedress
signals sun to set.
my father's planting sprawls thicklimbed and sound.
tomorrow. some stranger will pass and ask
                    how did he break this unfriendly ground?

Angeline, Daughter of Alcie

mother, you were going to run away
it would be a dark room of other peoples breath
and colors to float against your discontent
my cousin who wore red dresses above her knees
before the fashion made you brave with her
a silence of no childrens need, a dark of no plaintives
calling

the two of you took the street in finery for
a sunday matinee

i was watching the sun alone and the distance taking you
        and touching my chiffon
        desolate

at the corner you turned and called my name
our cousin shook her head because you were not brave

you could not bear a child of yours alone
bear anything that was not to share

hopeless, my cousin shaking her head, while i
ran to walk with you where you were

mother, you are chronic, hopelessly a lover, i fear
even now,
watching my self changing in the face of fools

it is congenital

Willie Mae

Willie Mae, she say he say:
Willie, you too nice a lookin
woman to cuss the way you do.

Goddamit, she say, fierce blue tongued,
who are you? Nobody
in forty years part me from my mouth.
      Not mama, daddy, minister.
This a package deal. You
don't take nothin out.

Everything she lay her mouth on turn
blue and beautiful and true.

(Do you remake the sun to
answer its warm darkening? Or
tamper with moon, or turn
its tide?)

Leave me alone and love me.
Leave me alone and love me.)

Cook County Hospital, 1962

Mysteriously swollen glands at ten.
I was on complete bed
rest, the nurses wrote in my
chart which I read
"seems content with bed
rest"
I read books (school, comic, anything)
all day long, uncomplaining.

At ten thirty at night
to the tin heartbeat of a radio
in the imperfect hotel quiet
of the hospital
I got out of bed
to dance
the Mashed Potatoes, furiously.

Down the hall death was murmuring
through the heavy mucus of a
child's throat.

Make/n My Music

my colored childhood was mostly music
      celebrate/n be/n young and Black (but we din know it)
          scream/n up the wide alleys
      an holler/n afta the walla-melon-man.

      sun-rest time
      my mama she wuz yell/n
          (all ova the block
               sang/n fa us
         ta git our butts in
             side).

we grew up run/n jazz rhythms
      and watch/n mr. wiggins downstairs
          knock the blues up side   his woman's
                  head.
we rocked.   and the big boys they snuck
an rolled   dice/   in the hallways at nite.

I mean. we laughed love.   an the teen
      agers they jus slow dragged thru smokey
                  tunes.
          life wuz a ordinary miracle   an
          have/n fun wuzn no temptation.

          we just dun it.
an   u know
I think we grew.   thru them spirit-uals
          the saint-tified folks wud git happy off
          of even if we wuz jus clown/n

when we danced the grizzly bear an
felt good when the reverend
with the black cadillac   said:

let the holy ghost come in
side you
that music make you/feel sooo/good!

any how   I wuz a little colored girl
                 then . . .

so far
my Black woman/hood ain't been noth/n but music

          i found billie
                 holiday   an learned
                             how
                             to cry.

a summer story

she dragged me from the backyard
all dirt and blacken/d further from sun.
from chianese changeling child
she made me a lady.
washed me pressed me slick in bangs
that slanted more my eyes. didn she say
i had those o/riental eyes?
starched me in a white dress made of stiff cloud.
the one i first communion/d in. she
scrubbed me and rubbed me
vaselined me a skin of brownshine.
she even made my knees
knees again. turned knobs of earth and ash.

she stood back.
in tired triumph and faced me
to a mirrorgirl
"now smile and show yo pretty big dimples!"

wasn't i the most beautiful charming
creature
a toughhand/ed and love armed cousin
ever made?

Memories/ The Red Bootee

for Mama

In the back of the drawer
(the important drawer—
where Mama and Madaddy kept
important things like
    birth certificates
    life insurance
    and
    all our old report cards)
In the back of the important
drawer where all the
important things (to be saved)
were kept—

we found a little biddy
red bootee
Tiny/leather/and trimmed
in fur/older than us.

A little red bootee.

And Mama said
it was Emma Lee's

a baby sister
older than us

who we'd never
even
seen.

I Break My Own Heart

I break my own heart now listening
my father talks me up at the head
of the long unbroken stair
 standing there
 braided, at midnight
 awake, waiting for his homecoming

praise for my pajamas with
fishes on them
and my sugar better than
Rose

So my father tells the scene in
the kitchen I don't remember my mother doesn't
either, but my bones stand

still at the top of the unbreaking
stair at midnight, awaiting

not father now home retired from the late
shift
his shoulders touching two walls
arising

the Sugar-man, the shoulderblade, the collar
bone, of impending strength who knows and I know him

who says my kiss unfolds sweeter, sweeter, sweeter,
than Rose
even

my fish swimming in their smells

                    in my unsleeping body

are the envy
of all seas
he has seen

if i tole you

(it's all so silly)
if i tole you
you'd laugh.

                    if i tole you
                    my body contained spirit
                    less than twenty
                    yrs.   but

                    i'm mo ancient
                    than age.

you'd laugh

                    at
                    longing.   distant as
                    an african sunset
                    in me.
                         this pregnant craving
                    for some unknown
                    fruit.   tired
                    thirsting an ancestral
                           drink
                    mo ancient
                    than age.   in me.
                    the feeling of an
                    emptiness in secret
                    holes that go unfilled
                           for a time
                    mo ancient
                    than age.   in me.

                    if i tole you   the
                    warm need blowin
                    restless.   in me.   mo
                    ancient than age.

you'd laugh
i know   and call it
                    growing pain.   (it's all
                    so silly.
                                you know)

and you'd
    laugh   if i tole you.   pains
                    ain't pains but ex-panding
                    spirits movin
                    in me.   movin to someplace
                                whose name i
                                        forgot
                    goin   somewhere mo
                    ancient than age.
                    in me.

if i tole you
            to   come.
                    and remember me
                    with me . . .
if i tole you
you'd laugh   like you did
                    before
                    those times
                        mo ancient than age
                        to me.

Second Meeting

memba the time . . .
　　　　　we met at home
　　that slow age ago.　　one day.
me.
　　　　with a water jar balanced
　　　　　　on my head
　　　　　　to fetch from the river
　　　　　　　　　and u
　　　　　　　　　and u wuz
　　　　hone/n a spear for the
　　　　hunt　　that nite
　　　　do u think about/—when
　　　　　　　　we'd met befo
　　　　　　in a　　/once life.　　one nite.
we shared the bitter ripe/ness
　　　　　　　　　　　of a
　　　　　　mango/　　　togetha
　　　　moved a　　　fertility dance
　　　　　　　beneath the warm east sky . . .
　　　　but i guess/　u forgot . . . till
　　　　　　　　　　we met　　again.
　　　　　　　　in this cold/　place
chicago.　　　the subway.
　　　like:
　　　　　　hey sista　　　wuts happen/n
　　　. . . and
　　　i reminded
　　　　u　　　　in a smile

don't i know u
        from
                sum/
                        where??
                                        u said. and
i nod/ed softly: yes.
                afraid I'd tip/ ova
                the water jar
        i always think
                is
                        balanced
                on my head . . .

Angel

for Jerry Ward

I am the only one here.

I stand in my one place
and I can see a good piece
down the road. I am yonder,
further than the chunk of your stone.
Right now, directly,
I am persimmon falling free
and the prisoner opening up
in me.
Don't come through my door and
want to run my house. I am
the angel who sweep air in and out my own
dancing body. I got good eyes. I can see.
A good piece down the road. Clear to
God murmuring in me. My head is the burning
bush. What I hold in my hand is the promised
land. I set my people free in me.
And we walk without wandering like people named
after mere plants,
because we are tree
and high-stepping roots
cake-walking
in this promised place.

Where I go is where I am now.
Don't mess with me: you hurt yourself.

In the middle of my stride now. I am walking
yes indeed I am walking through my own house.
I am walking yes indeed on my own piece of road.
Toting my own load
and yours and mine.
I tell you
I feel fine and clear this morning even
when it's night and a full moon with my thumbprint
on it.
Everything is clamorous and quiet.
> I am the only One here.
> And we don't break. No indeed.
> Come hell and high water.
> We don't break
> for nothing.

Veneration: Maturity

African-American Woman Guild

Mary Mariah Jefferson Jackson, Greenville, Mississippi
Born 1885(?)
Alcie Turner Robinson, Los Angeles, California
Born 1902
Angeline Robinson Jackson, Chicago, Illinois
Born 1921

Bird, pick up your bones
from the bed. Untwine
your joints and your
spine. Release the blood
that tries to knot you
in your mind. Oh, Flight!   Mother
Memory.

Spider, retrace the
wisdom you have
woven.
The Blues you trapped
and ate
in the corners of
your haunted house
between your legs
in the birthplace.

You thicken in your middle.
You saved edibles for this winter.
You are no girl. Squandering.

And your breasts
hide what they
know. Keep close
to you like
memory.
Snake-sister, whose hair
spins pale
and skin buckles
at the worn-weave.
Receive new cloth. Oh,
Light! Excellent-luminous.
Shining in dark patterned
coat.

Here it is.
You think that time is running
out.
When Time is running
in.

george, after all, means farmer

he carried a tomato plant &
watermelon
across the daydream highways and no stop sign ever touched him
he would not wait
there is one line in the palm
of his hand
it is thick as blood and crooked and crowded
against calluses
one line that is heart and life and a head

elaborate as the green that stalks into soft red moons

ambiguous bleeding that wants to be fruit
& vegetable
the way insanity wants genius save for cruelty

and this is in his hand
the bloodline let loose

his caring is locked into the soil
and some days i believe i must leave it there

it is most sure of itself
when red roses unpeel and threaten the discipline of winters
my father's flesh indelible

hunched over a handplow
in eulogy for his father's flesh, in fear
that all of his line would waste like a water-
melon flung against the earth

and the meat broken from tenderness
& bleeding in splits like fruit too soft from too much sun

too long a time alone gray
he hunches against the handplow, he is turning to gray and metal

as if he has known his earth's cruelty
a long long time

One Kitchen

for Angeline, Emma, and Alcie

"How you cookin that, girl?"
"Don't you snap your beans before you—? Don't you
sautee your onions before you—? They taste so much
better." My mother, at our last supper, asked me. While
she, under my squinting gaze,
failed to wrap the fish red in silver foil; instead
fed it naked, full of bread and herbs, to the oven.
I wrinkled my face at her unfinessed method. She
(who invented all food; she who invented all art;
she who invented mirrors) prayed for days
when I stood awed at her elbow watching her bend
fire up and down, break greens, and lengthen roots,
with no mind of my own: her own idea solid beside
her on each one of her breaths, hanging. Now

how does it feel to be a woman with a mother and
her own ways; or mother, how does it feel to be
a mother with a daughter and her own style? Speak to me,
Woman.

You are my favored child.

One Quasi-Sonnet from the Portuguese

*In the photo, the Portuguese soldier stood with the head of the Angolan
in hand.*

Why he of the nightmare-slew remember
Who tore through the bush till we took his hand
That one squat fellow, arms thick as timber
Fitting to lead us to his brothers'·band?
We followed his vein-red tracks best we might
In mud's mouth he leapt (lips laughed like his race)
After the torn body bolted from sight
With rifle butt I wiped away his face.

Like a tree thick arms take root in my brain
This squat gore from my true foreign fable:
Remember his screams: falling Negro rain.
He: head white teeth and eye, aged and able.
The rest are voices in an unknown tongue
Stripped from a child's throat in sun hanging.
    Hung.

       1974–1986

a beginning for new beginnings

and some where distantly
there is an answer
      as surely as this breath
      half hangs befo my face
and some where
there is a move meant.
      as certain as the wind
      arrives and departs
      from me.
and always.

there is a struggling to be
and constantly
our voices rise. in silent straining
      to be free . . .
and some where
there is an answer. a How.
that I can feel and be felt in. and live
within a Reason
and a Way
and some time

there is a Morning
the rise of an Other Day.
(but the Fight
is in the wading. waiting
out this night.
the Fight is in the living thru
till mornings rise

close/d and secure in u.)
but this time.
our eyes cannot see
and the night lends no helping hand.
the waters of this land
are freezing.
still.
i. and we. struggle.
and we float.

children. together. (u. me. she. and us. and him.)
together. children.
we learn How
to swim.

Haiti: 1979

This is the land of heartbreak and fever,
invisible police and brokenteeth and back.
This is the red flower land opening out
our veins. This is the pull in the arteries;
the art of the moment under sun: a sugar drink
in a hazy bottle on a cart in the corner of
the crying eye. This is the place of the hungry
hawker who swoops around demanding we hold and
honor his wares and blackbirds who brushed death
with the edges of their wings swinging over
into the wide canyons we careen along an eyelash
distance from infinity.
This is the funeral walking sober the side of the road.
Turn our eyes away in reverence and sorrow from the gray
casket and the weepers with desert eyes, dry without
a drink of tears.

And this land scalds the lookers and the empty
touchers come away with pieces of art and I
come away with pieces of a heart.

*

Henri Christophe walks across the avenue. Midday.
He opens his mouth and swallows. Despair?

This sadness here is beyond me. This begging
in the streets. It should reach a point of rage
of no return.

This begging in the streets they own.
I am tired for us. For the 47th Street of this.
Disrepair. For the places of ill-repute in which eyes
stare out at me staring back at me at my own
polite swallowing.

But we have our gods and let them bless me
even as I say what good are they if they do
not push us as they did before—to burn
the overseers seeing nothing but their own
fingers lacquered plowing the cane face of this
port au prince of storm and saying nothing to the ocean
awaiting the speech of the fishermen and the hills
wanting the farmer's hand to pray for us all.

Have you a memory of the fire in the hills?

I am told that those elevated by voudon at some time
can handle fire without its burn: I have watched
a woman talking like a man, sitting like a man,
pouring rum like a man, I watched her eat fire
and tell me my complete secret. Her house was so poor
and occupying earth like a vague afterthought. But clean
as water I have dreamed through. I believed that her
gods were mine that they will scorch through you like
rum and knock you down and ride you like a horse
and let men dance with fire wrapped around their penises.
But where is the memory of the fire in the hills?

And we are no better no worse. We are all beggars.
A-begging what is ours. A-begging what is yours and mine
once you have been born human and intercoursed with gods
eye to eternal, inner eye. Never setting.
Like a fire in a hill.

Poems from FESTAC '77

*The Second World Black and African Festival of Arts and Culture,
Lagos, Nigeria*

for Abena, Joyce, the North American Zone Committee

the ways we will deny ourselves

---

feeling at last returns to dust
the
bones fold a
    way
blood diverges

and can never be together
again
in this exact narrow

cross
road

we could say it was a dream (only
        cloud and irresistible
        heat)

easier
than shaping what is now

one slip of the tongue

an oval of four we sat
one nativeborn alone inside his accent
two women from the states silent in smiles

"i cain't tell one
            from the other." the u.s.
            brother.
"all these turkeys look alike."

the nigerian slipped behind a mask

slow a shame sank round us all
sad
birds of a feather
don't always recognize
            each other.

parentage

---

say only we are children
who grew up far away
(every child has a mother, has a
father)

my mother is this continent is a
theater
of labor, stricken, touched, is howls is
pain of birth and celebration

my father as yours is
                    distant convocation, is
waterfront and wharf
where ships unload, re
sources, disembark a people
set down
wise and willful, full of changes

i was conceived in a place not far
from here

Flags

"miss," he said,
"i watched you. moving in the
parade. i like the way you move. i want
to satisfy your movement."

here i thought my body
was a banner, a flag unfurled diaspora
across the sky

a purely political spread.

he imagined me in bed.

steveland

women gathered wings and
flew
over sand to touch stevie wonder's
hand.
as best we could
we froze him in cubes of light

for he was water, elusive
even always there

listening to voices over his shoulder
spirits alight
and hugging him

circling us for a song.

A Wedding Reception

Family arguments
in another language not firsthand, cousins
we come several times removed, we are curious
relations come to visit, bring
ceremony, bridge a breach
of birth and incomplete
burial.

Every courtesy is ours. Strife
is swept under the rug of ragged edges.
Bamboo
shades are hung. Somewhere
fresh sugar cane is cut, palms
wave
as we
stroll thru the aisles of the city
ushers with magazines

and guns
make a way for us
brides and grooms.

People greet us with a mixed
blessing, handshakes and stares.

Our beds are made, and shades are
drawn, the best wine is drunk,
beer and plaintains
served.

We lie in air thick as bridal
bouquet.

We join inside the Ancestor's womb.

While family argues, distant,
furious,
in the backroom.

What I Said as a Child

What I said as a child I say
as a woman:

>   There is romance in common
>   movement
>   of sound and sand.
>   Religion of a
>   kind is
>   true, affirmed.

>   Ours is the worn water and ripe fire, leaves
>   that burn alongside the road
>   into
>   smoke
>   thick as Nigerian oil. A cover
>   for
>   magic and skill.

>   We balanced a house of extended families
>   atop our heads.
>   The music drifted down
>   around our faces.
>   Wind crossed our cheeks
>   in scarifications.
>   Spirits feathered around our waists
>   and fell to our knees;
>   a dance of prayers that I said as a child

I say again:

>   We walked in the air of the ancestors,
>   hot and tight